Adventures with JONNY

Ice Fishing!
The Coolest Sport on Earth

A parent and child ice fishing adventure and guide

Michael DiLorenzo

Illustrated By Jenniffer Julich

Running Moose Publications, Inc.
Clinton Township, Michigan

Printed in Singapore

Jonny says...Ice Safety First!

Before venturing out on the ice with your children, have them put on a properly fitting personal floatation device (pfd) under their winter coats. A vest-style pfd should fit comfortably under most bulky winter coats and will keep them afloat in the event of an accident.

Regardless of the adventure you are embarking upon with your children, remember Safety First, Adventure Second!

Published by Running Moose Publications, Inc.
42400 Garfield Road
Clinton Township, MI 48038

Publisher's Cataloging-in-Publication Data
DiLorenzo, Michael.

Adventures with Jonny: ice fishing! The coolest sport on Earth / Michael DiLorenzo. –
Clinton Township, MI: Running Moose Publications, 2006.

p.; cm.
ISBN: 0-9777210-1-9
ISBN13: 978-0-9777210-1-6

1. Ice fishing. 2. Ice fishing--Equipment and supplies. I. Title.

SH455.45 .D55 2006
799.12/2—dc22   2006936721

Book production and coordination by Jenkins Group, Inc. • www.bookpublishing.com
Cover and interior illustrations by Jenniffer Julich
Layout by Eric Tufford

Printed in Singapore
11 10 09 08 07 • 5 4 3 2 1

 This book is first and foremost dedicated...

...to my family, without whom there would be no adventure!

Beyond family, this book is dedicated to the mentors of the outdoor world, those of you who have put aside your own ambitions to take a child and walk him or her through their initial outdoor experience. Regardless of the success of your early outings, this introduction alone will lead many children to a lifelong journey of outdoor adventures.

I have been fortunate to have had many mentors in my life, from my father and his friends to some of my own friends and their fathers. Those who have taken the time to introduce a new facet of the outdoors to me have left an indelible mark.

Mentoring is an ongoing process, as outdoor pursuits continually evolve and so do the participants. Mentoring does not have to apply to youth alone. Many adolescents or adults have yet to catch their first fish or go on their first hunt. Age often numbs peoples' willingness to venture out on their own, despite their level of interest, but I believe it is never too late to share the outdoors with someone.

Mentoring can be addicting, as the reward of reliving your inaugural outdoor experiences through another's eyes invigorates your own passions. Though many say "Take a kid fishing," I say "Take anyone fishing" and see who gets hooked!

Why did I create Jonny?

The writing of this book, the development of Jonny, and the basis of the Adventures with Jonny series is to introduce young children to outdoor adventures that can become a key part of their lives to be enjoyed forever. If you as a parent can give your child the gift of the outdoors, you will give him or her a gift for life.

The pace of today's society, the burden of too many structured youth activities, and the ravenous consumption of our children's time by television, video games, and computers denies them the opportunity to experience all that awaits them in the world of outdoor pursuits. To run without a coach, to play without instruction, and to learn without a lesson plan are but a few of the many benefits that outdoor adventures can provide to our children.

I hope that more families will once again grasp the value of the outdoor experience and recognize the traditions that can be built together around regular outdoor adventures.

The outdoor experiences you share together will no doubt create some of your fondest memories and establish themselves as building blocks of your parent/child relationship, as they have done for my family and me.

Please enjoy this book with your children, and take them fishing when you're done.

Fish on!

Photo by Laura DiLorenzo

Table of Contents

that the lakes would freeze up
for some hard water fishing

Winter brings a lot of fun
but nothing is so nice

as gathering with my friends

and going fishing
through the ice

First we go see Tackle Tommy
to get our hooks and bait
He tells us what to use
so our fishing will be great

Watching, all excited
    while snowflakes touch our lips
Dad finishes the holes
    and we scoop out the chips

For **BIG** fish like pike, we set out a tip-up

When the fish bites the bait, a flag will then FLIP UP!

Then we run across the ice
and I *SLIDE* on my fanny

11

going towards my dad
   who's now setting up our shanty

Baiting up
our rods
using cool-
looking jigs

hoping fish
will come along
and chow down our ICE RIGS

13

Taking pictures of our catch everybody is excited
This is all so much fun we are thoroughly delighted

Sliding back to our shanty
to count the fish we have, "That's enough for dinner!"
I shout out to my dad

Parents' "How-to" Fishing Guide
Adventure Tips for Parents

Getting to Know Your Ice: The Cold, Hard Truth

One thing I have learned over the years is that many people have an inherent fear of the ice. They assume there is no such thing as safe ice and discount ice fishermen as life-risking morons. Therefore, many individuals, including summertime fishermen, cheat themselves of the experience for fear of a bone-chilling bath. Well, believe me, no ice fisherman wants to take a cool dip anymore than you do, but they have learned to discern safe ice from unsafe ice and confidently go about their winter pursuits in search of fish.

Assuming you have no experience with ice at all, there is no sense in running out on the season's first ice to try this type of fishing, especially with your children in tow. Wait for the ice to solidly develop before you try your first venture. Unfortunately, there is no set timeframe for how long it takes a body of water to freeze in the area you will be fishing. There are just too many factors affecting how quickly and safely a body of water will develop safe ice conditions.

You must take into consideration many variables for each given body of water. Any inlets or outlets of a lake generally have some flow or current in those areas that can cause unsafe early ice. In fact, if there is enough of a current, safe ice may never develop in such spots. Also, springs in the floor of the lake may cause unsafe ice conditions above them, depending on how deep they lie below the surface. Any body of water that has a current to it will freeze much slower than still water that has no current. Some very slow-flowing rivers will produce safe ice, but many never will, and although they may eventually ice over, truly safe ice may never develop. A river is the last place I would venture out on if I were uncertain of the ice conditions. Falling through the ice with a current below can be a recipe for disaster.

Also, if you will be fishing a lake whose water level is controlled by a dam, be certain the ice has not been compromised by a recent adjustment or release of water from the dam.

The Freezing Process

Besides the fact that it just has to be really cold outside, it helps to understand how a body of water actually freezes. Basic Science 101: cold temperatures fall while warm temperatures rise, and so it goes for water as well. As the air becomes frigid, the surface water cools and sinks to the bottom, pushing warmer water towards the surface. This cycle repeats itself again and again until the surface temperature reaches a constant freezing point. This is when ice begins to develop. With this freezing process in mind, it makes sense that a shallow body of water will turn over much quicker and thus freeze earlier than a deep body of water. A shallow lake or pond may freeze weeks ahead of a neighboring deeper lake.

Thunder and Lightning

One last science lesson: what happens to water when it freezes? It expands. While the ice is continuing to develop, the expansion causes pressure cracks that resound through the ice with a thunderous drone. Typically, on days that are well below freezing, this sound may occur regularly and can be quite loud. It is not uncommon to actually see the cracks run across the surface of the ice like a streak of lightning or for the water to move slightly in the hole that you are fishing as a result in the relief of water pressure below the ice. While this noise and movement may take some getting used to, they do not mean the ice is unsafe. Remember, ice floats, so it will not crack and sink to the bottom. Also, if you are in a small body of water that is completely frozen over, there is no place for the ice to go or for a piece to break off and float away.

A pressure crack may be as minimal as a subtle, crooked line below the surface of the ice or may actually develop a separation as wide as a few inches at the surface of the ice and run for several hundred yards. Again, if you are on a small, completely frozen body of water, there is no place for the ice to go so an ice floe will not result from the pressure crack. However, if you are fishing on a large body of water or a bay off a larger lake that has not frozen all the way across, a large pressure crack can result in an ice floe, especially if it is accompanied by an offshore wind. Should these conditions arise, get onto the land side of the pressure crack immediately. In these conditions, it would not be unusual for a large ice floe to develop. An ice floe can begin as large as a mile across or larger, but as it floats out to sea, depending on winds and waves, it breaks up into smaller pieces of ice, eventually becoming too small to support the weight of a fisherman. I don't care if fish are jumping out of the hole or you're fishing in very shallow water, get safely back on land. They're just fish, and compromising your safety or worse yet, your child's safety, is not worth it. Any of these fish are just ten dollars a pound down at the local market if you want them that much.

How Thick Is Thick Enough?

Here is a general rule of thumb as far as ice thickness is concerned: three inches of ice is safe to support an average adult's weight and eight inches of ice will support an all-terrain vehicle (ATV) such as a snowmobile or four-wheeler that many ice fishermen use to transport themselves and their gear to their ice-fishing destinations. These are conservative numbers, as many will argue that a mere two inches of early ice will safely support an adult. I'm not stopping those who have this belief, but with kids in tow and fluctuations in ice thickness, I would prefer to err on the side of caution.

Safe for an ATV

Safe for an adult

Jonny

28

The Ice Age

Much like people, age degrades the strength of ice. Early ice will generally freeze up very clear and solid, lacking air bubbles or debris that can cloud the ice. In many lakes, you can actually see through the early ice to the bottom as if you were walking on a giant sheet of glass. This very clear ice can give you a sense of uneasiness, but it is normally very strong and very safe. As ice ages and warm spells come and go throughout the winter months, ice tends to become porous, developing an internal honeycomb pattern. Consequently, towards the end of the season (also called "last ice"), even a foot of old ice may render itself unsafe.

A Blanket of Snow

We've all heard the term "blanket of snow," and no truer words have ever been spoken when it comes to the development of safe versus unsafe ice. The word "blanket" gives the feeling of warmth or insulation, and that is exactly what happens when snow falls on early ice. The ice becomes blanketed or sheltered from the cold air above, and as a result, the freezing process slows down. So if a lake has just begun to freeze over and then gets a solid blanket of snow on top, it will take much longer for safe ice to develop underneath the snow. This is just one other factor to take into consideration when determining whether ice is safe.

Up Comes the Water on Unsafe Ice

During early season ice fishing, you may punch a hole through the ice and then notice the water slowly pushing up through the hole and spreading out on the surface. Though the ice on which you are standing may feel solid, your weight is actually pushing the ice downward and thus forcing water up through the hole you have opened. This is a very good indication that you need to venture elsewhere. While this may just be a weak area in that immediate spot and safe ice may be but a few hundred feet away, this is no area from which to safely ice fish.

R.E.S.P.E.C.T. the Water in All Forms

None of this is meant to scare you or dampen your enthusiasm for ice fishing, but just as boaters have to respect the water to safely enjoy their sport, so too must ice fishermen respect the ice and develop an understanding of its complexities and the effects of nature on the development of safe ice. So here's the gig: until you are confident enough to set out on the ice on your own, you may be more comfortable going with others you know who are seasoned ice fishermen. If you are a first-timer, you might feel more comfortable going on a kid-free venture first to get comfortable with the whole ice fishing thing. This will help you to develop confidence in the ice conditions and make your initial venture with your children more enjoyable. Fishing buddies are great to have and I recommend bringing one along to share the experience with and to build your confidence in the safety of the ice. A cell phone also makes for a good safety item just in case.

Stay on Course/ATV Travel

Wind and a Compass

Most of your early outings will likely be very close to shore, but as you gain confidence in ice

29

conditions and your ice fishing skills, you will begin to venture further out. The further you venture from shore, the more you need to have a dependable compass with you. You may think this sounds odd, since you can readily see the shore from quite a distance out onto the lake, but ice typically holds some snow on its surface. If a gusty wind suddenly starts blowing, it can quickly make good vision a thing of the past. Once your visibility is obscured, it can be very difficult to ascertain your sense of direction and tell which route is the way back to shore and your vehicle.

Likewise, if you will be traveling any distance from shore, it is a good idea to take a compass reading before you begin your trek so you will know in which direction to return should you lose visibility while on your outing.

ATV Travel Should Be a Slow Go

If you will be traveling out on the ice by means of a snowmobile or ATV such as a four-wheeler, it is safest to travel at a slow to moderate speed. You will already be reaching your destination more quickly than if you were walking, so go slowly and keep safety in mind.

Avoid snowdrifts that could be masking a large pressure crack or ice chunk removed from a shanty hole. Blowing snow will drift against anything that breaks its path, including ice that has shelved up upon itself or blocks of ice removed from a shanty hole. If you blindly travel through snowdrifts, something could be lying in wait to greet you, so it's best to avoid large drifts if you can or else traverse through them slowly.

Open Holes

Keep an eye out for open fishing holes left by fishermen who have recently been fishing in the area. For the most part, these holes do not pose a safety threat, since most range in size from six to ten inches across. However, this size hole is just big enough for a small foot to fall through and cause a chilly foot or leg soaker, quickly bringing your outing to a close. Keep in mind that some fishermen occasionally cut a very large hole to be used when spear fishing in a shanty. These larger holes will present a danger to your children and possibly even to you depending upon the ambition of the angler who cut the hole. Common ice courtesy would be to mark the open hole with a stick or branch brought from shore to alert other anglers of the hole, but since common courtesy is sometimes not so common, keep an eye out for your safety and don't forget to mark your own holes once you have finished fishing for the day.

Stick with the Crowds

In the beginning, you will feel more confident fishing with the masses. As I have said before, ask lots of questions at the local sporting goods stores or even in the parking areas near the water about the conditions of the ice, where unsafe ice may exist, and where people are having the most success on the ice. As your confidence grows, you can begin to venture away from the pack and strike out on your own. The drawback to fishing in the crowd is that noise generated by packs of fishermen can spook the fish and stop them from biting.

Test As You Go

One of the first pieces of equipment you should have in your possession is an ice spud. This is a steel pole, typically five to six feet in length, with a flattened chisel tooth business end. The spud is generally

used for punching holes through the ice, but it doubles as a great piece of safety equipment to test the ice as you walk. The spud should have a loop of rope at the handle that should always be around your wrist when testing the ice. Should you hit a thin patch of ice where the spud shoots through on the first hit, or as you finish a hole should the spud slip from your hands, the rope loop will keep it from becoming a lost treasure at the bottom of the lake.

Test the ice by striking down hard with the spud. In safe ice conditions, the spud will chip the surface ice away and that's about it. If the spud breaks through the ice in one punch, hit the road, because the ice is just not safe in that area. If you can, double back on the tracks you came in on, just in case there is other unsafe ice in the immediate area. Continually test the ice as you walk and randomly test the ice in the area you will be fishing before you let your kids run about.

Ice Spud

Safe-T First

Before venturing out on the ice, teach your children this lesson. Should anybody ever fall through the ice, make like a "T" and spread your arms out wide. This will prevent the person from going under the ice and keep them at the surface until help arrives.

Ice Tips

Short and Sweet

The key to a successful introduction to ice fishing is to keep the trips short, especially if your child hints at being cold. You will have much greater success on several very short trips with your kids than holding them hostage on a frozen tundra when they are not having fun. Also, if the fish do not seem to be particularly cooperative on your outing, pack it up and try again another day.
Do not overstay your welcome if the fish do not want to play.

Fall Down, Go Boom!

Though it may not hurt your kids to have a close encounter with the ice, as an adult, you're going to want to avoid this as much as possible. First of all, take short steps and do not extend your stride so that the point of your heel comes down to strike the ice in front of you. Instead, try to walk as flatfooted as possible, as this will help to keep you on your feet and off your keester.

Jeepers Peepers, Where'd You Get Those...Creepers!

Creepers are a great piece of safety equipment and one of the most important items you can add to your collection of outdoor gear. Creepers are metal spikes or springs that attach to the bottoms of your boots and prevent you from sliding on the ice. While they come in many designs, I suggest looking for a pair that covers the entire bottom of your boot as opposed to models that fit only in front of the heel portion of your boot and do not cover the heel of your sole.

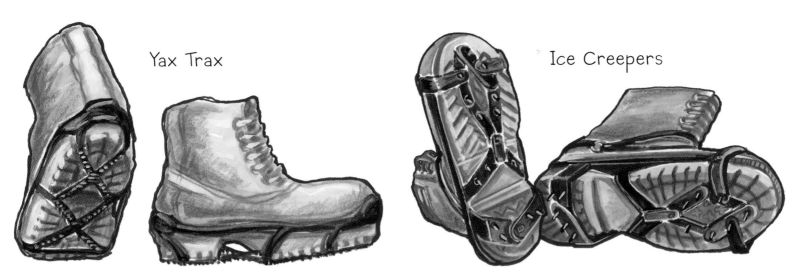

Yax Trax

Ice Creepers

Newer models of creepers resemble a rubber web intertwined through a series of springs. This design provides additional traction across the entire bottom of the boot and allows you to walk more naturally than other creeper models. However, some of these creepers have a tendency to slip off your boot as you walk. This can be remedied by hooking a small bungee cord across the top of your boot to each side of the creeper.

Safety Spikes or Nails

Hopefully you will never have to use them, but in the event of an emergency, safety spikes or nails are vital to have on hand. Safety spikes are a pair of plastic handles with a metal spike protruding from one end of each handle connected with a length of cord long enough to hang from your neck and reach down to your wrists. In the event that you break through the ice, these provide the vital grip you need to pull yourself from the ice. Without these, it is virtually impossible to pull yourself from the ice as the water creates such a slippery surface that you simply cannot get the grip and balance you need to extract yourself from the water. I have carried mine around for years, and thanks to good judgement, have not had occasion to use them yet.

Safety Spikes

Getting Dressed for the Occasion

The key to staying warm in any cold weather activity is to dress in layers. This goes for both you and your children. Avoid wearing cotton next to the skin as it does not have much in the way of insulating value and damp cotton will draw heat from your body. I suggest starting with long underwear made from synthetic fabric that wicks moisture from your skin when you perspire. Most people don't think about sweating during the winter months, but you can work up quite a sweat while walking on the ice, pulling your sled, and cutting your fishing holes.

After the base layer, I like to wear a turtleneck with a snug collar to keep out unwanted back drafts. Complete this with a heavy sweatshirt, polar fleece jacket, or heavy flannel shirt. For a jacket, naturally a heavily insulated winter coat that has a tough outer shell to break the wind is preferred. I prefer a coat to a jacket as a jacket will lift up when you sit down and expose your waist to cool breezes. To avoid overheating at the start of your adventure, I suggest keeping your coat open or packing your coat with

your gear and placing it on your sled for the walk out. Once you have arrived at your destination and have cut your holes, your heavy work will be done and you can put your coat on to stay warm. Although I suggest this for you, keep the coats on the kids as their tolerance to the cold is normally not the same as adults.

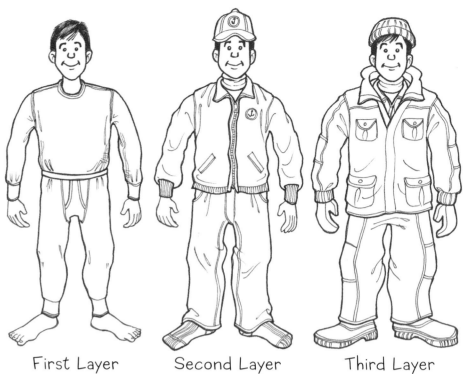

First Layer   Second Layer   Third Layer

To keep your legs warm, I again suggest some type of long johns composed of synthetic material to help wick moisture from your skin. Insulated underwear comes in a variety of weights and everyone has a different tolerance for the cold, so wear whatever makes you comfortable. I follow this up with a regular pair of jeans and waterproof ski pants or bibs to break the wind and keep my legs dry, as I often find myself kneeling on the ice. If you are a hunter, you can use the same warm gear you use in the woods. You don't need to have a special outfit for every activity, and ice fishing is certainly no fashion show.

Don't ignore the feet. Our extremities are always the first to get cold. Definitely avoid cotton if you can and wear one good thick pair of wool socks. Wool, unlike cotton, retains warmth even when damp. Many people make the mistake of tugging on a second pair of socks and then jamming their feet into their boots. Feet need to breathe to stay warm, and having some room in your boot to create a warm pocket of air around your feet will help keep them warm and happy.

Dress your kids the same way you dress yourself. Their comfort will be the determining factor in your length of stay during your ice fishing adventures.

Our heads are our bodies' chimneys, and more heat escapes from the head than any other area of the body. A heavy warm hat is a must for you and your children. Again, to avoid overheating, you may want to wear just a ball cap on the walk out and save your heavy hat for when you're set up and fishing.

Gloves. Bring extras, period! Children cannot avoid the temptation to slide on the ice or stick their hands in the holes or somehow get their hands wet. Bring along plenty of extra gloves. If your kids have waterproof gloves, these will certainly help but they too have limits. You may even want an extra pair for yourself should you dampen a glove.

If you and your children enjoy the sport and can see more ice fishing in your future, then watch the end-of-the-season sales for deep discounts on warm winter wear. Having the proper gear to stay warm will make this and any other winter activity more enjoyable for everyone. Just remember to buy some items a bit bigger for your kids as they will grow like grass throughout the summer.

33

Let's Go Fishing!

Play Twenty Questions

You can never ask enough questions when it comes to fishing, including ice fishing. While buying your bait or tackle supplies, ask these specific questions:

- **What lake has recently been good for ice fishing?**
- **Where on the lake are fish being caught?**
- **In how deep of water are fish being caught?**
- **How far below the ice are fish being caught?**
- **What bait is being used?**
- **What lures or jigs are being used?**
- **What color bait has been most productive?**
- **What time of day has fishing been most productive?**

When you arrive at the lake that you intend to fish, talk with other ice fishermen at the parking area or as you come upon them on your walk out on the ice.

Look for Active Fishermen

A picture is worth a thousand words. This also applies to good ice fishing. If you see crowds of ice fishermen in one spot, it does not necessarily mean they are catching fish. Within this crowd, if you see several fishermen standing around in conversation, most likely the only thing biting is the wind.

The Arms Have It!

One consistent way to spot fishermen actively catching fish is by the motion of their arms. If you see lots of arm activity, specifically arms moving quickly overhead, you are in an area with actively feeding fish. Set up in this area and start fishing.

The Ears Have It!

If you come across a village of shanties cooped together on the ice, there is a reason they are all in the same spot. As you walk around the shanties, listen closely for conversations inside or any hootin' and hollerin' that might be taking place. A lot of guys just get too darned excited when they catch fish to contain their enjoyment. If you hear positive words, try fishing in that area as well.

The Eyes Have It!

When fish are actively biting, fishermen will not take time to neatly put away each fish they catch. While the bite is on, they will lay the fish around them on the ice and concentrate on fishing. This too is an obvious sign of good fish activity.

Same Place, Different Season

Beyond playing "Monkey See, Monkey Do," you should learn the proper way to find fish on your own during your ice fishing adventures. Use the same principles you would during the regular fishing season and look for places that have structure in the water. The places that hold fish in the spring,

34

summer, and fall will most likely hold them in the winter as well. Thus, the best place to start the ice season is the same place you caught fish in the late fall. Chances are, the area where fish were caught just before ice-up still holds fish, and keeping tabs on such an area prior to ice-up can also pay off. Drop-offs are key locations to concentrate your efforts, as are reefs and underwater shoals or other submerged structures such as weedbeds, stick piles, and rocks.

How Do You Find Them?

If you're an active summer fisherman, make a mental note of the area as best you can in relation to shoreline landmarks or, better yet, use a GPS to pinpoint areas on the water that hold fish during the summer and fall months. Otherwise, obtain a topographical map of the lake you are going to fish and look for areas of structure on the map.

One Good Hole Deserves Another

When you arrive at your fishing spot, punch a series of well spaced holes and try fishing each one until you find fish. If you're looking for a drop-off, clip a sinker to your bait and drop it to the bottom to quickly approximate the depth. Keep moving inward or outward and testing the water depth until you see a sharp change in depth. As with summer fishing, you will have better success fishing the deeper side of the drop-off or right at the edge of the drop-off if you can locate it exactly.

Once you have found active fish, you can get the gang fishing together by punching a number of holes close together and fishing on top of the school you have located. You can only fish one line per hole that you cut in the ice, as multiple lines fished in the same hole will tangle together and be difficult to untangle or retie in cold weather.

Like Birds on a Wire

If you have ever watched a flock of birds on a wire or in a tree, the flock stays together for a while, flies off, circles back, and then returns to its roost. Schools of fish have a tendency to do the same thing. They are nomadic in nature, and though you may be in the right area with good structure, the fish will move around during the day, even within minutes. Moving around quite a bit to initially locate fish is generally a good idea, but once you have found a good area, the fish activity may come and go. You can continue to move around in an effort to stay with the school, but you never know in which direction they are going to head. You might elect to just sit tight and wait for the school to return to your area. This too is an easier alternative than running your kids all over the ice. Just know that during your outing, you may incur moments of very active biting followed by complete inactivity, and this will be the tempo of that day.

Target Species

Fish for panfish (perch, bluegill, or crappie) for your inaugural fishing adventure with your children. They can be very cooperative and provide lots of action to keep your little adventurers intrigued during your outing. However, since big fish like to eat little fish and may very likely be in the area, bring along a tip-up (see page 43) or two on your outing and set them up for larger fish such as pike or walleye. The potential to catch a big fish adds an element of excitement to your outing and helps to hold your children's interest as they keep a watchful eye out in hopes of a flying flag. Pulling a large fish through the ice is just a ton of fun, but since they can be tougher to catch, I would not make it the sole focus of your early outings.

What Do I Need to Get Started?

Fishing License and Regulations Book

Most states require that adults have a fishing license, even when just fishing with children. If you purchased an annual fishing license for summer fishing, the license should still be good throughout the winter months. Nonetheless, check the expiration date on your license before your outing and always carry a current license with you.

When you purchase your license, you will receive a complimentary rule book from the state's Department of Natural Resources or the Ministry of Natural Resources if you are fishing in Canada. The book will inform you of the species that are in season during the winter months along with their size and catch limits. Most states do not require that a minor child have a separate fishing license, but children still must abide by the same fishing rules and regulations as adults. A fishing license can be picked up at most sporting goods stores or tackle shops.

Fishing Poles

Gone are the long rods of summer when it comes to winter's ice fishing pursuits. The standard ice rod will range in length from a stubby eighteen inches to a stretched out thirty-six inches with most averaging right around two feet in total length. Ice rods too will come in different actions with medium or heavy actions used for larger fish such as walleye or pike and light or ultra-light used for smaller game such as panfish, the target of our adventure. The reason such light rods are used for winter fishing is that panfish tend to bite very lightly in the winter and many would never be felt when using heavier rods.

Fishing Reels

There are essentially two forms of reels used in ice fishing: smaller fly-style reels for fishing shallower waters or small spinning reels for deeper waters. You can find fly reels in very small sizes to hold just the small amount of line that you need when fishing shallow lakes or ponds. There are even small, all-plastic reels that resemble a fly reel that are very lightweight and hold enough line to do the job. The fly reels I suggest are of the most basic design and feature. They are the smallest models available so as not to overwhelm the short rods of the ice season, and they are not the elaborate pricey models you may associate with lofty fly rod combinations. The use of a fly reel would only be suggested when fishing for panfish or other smaller fish that would not require the use of a drag system on the reel. If you are fishing for anything that may put up a fight or potentially pull line from the reel, use a spinning reel.

If you are using a standard fly reel, I suggest popping out the spool and wrapping the arbor in the middle of the spool with cork or some other bulky material to expand the arbor that the line will be wrapped upon inside the spool. The purpose of this is to avoid the very tight kinking that can occur in the fishing line when wrapped around the normally small arbor of a fly reel. You could also accomplish

this by purchasing very inexpensive backing line and first attaching this to the reel and then tying/connecting the actual fishing line to the backing line. The whole purpose of this is to aid in keeping the line as limber as possible and to avoid having the line come off the reel in a tight coil made even worse by the cold winter weather.

If you are using a spinning reel, I again suggest sticking to a smaller size so you don't overwhelm the short rods used for ice fishing. Select a reel that is just big enough to hold the amount of line necessary to perform the task at hand. You may have a spinning reel that you use on an ultra-light rod during the summer that will double as a dandy ice fishing reel as well.

Regardless of the style of reel you are using, reels have moving parts and therefore should never be set in the snow or on the surface of the ice where slush or moisture could get on or into the reel. Obviously, the moisture on or inside the reel will eventually freeze and render the reel useless. Upon your return home from your ice fishing adventure, store your rods/reels at least temporarily inside your house to allow them to warm and dry thoroughly so that you don't start your next adventure with frozen gear.

Fishing Line

Again, you have to select line for the task at hand and should always try to minimize the strength and diameter of the line selected. Water clarity can vastly improve within a body of water from summer to winter since wind and boat traffic can be factored out of the equation. Fish can be very fussy about feeding on baits with heavy strings attached. The fishing industry, always obliging sportsmen with an answer to our needs, produces a number of fishing lines specifically made for ice fishing. The primary advantages of these lines are their very small diameters and resiliency to cold weather as they have less tendency to tightly coil up than regular monofilament fishing lines. There are even braided "super" lines that are great for deep water jigging as they lack the elasticity of monofilament lines and thus any bites or bumps offered by fish are more easily felt by the angler at the other end of the line. Braided "super" lines also offer a significant strength to diameter ratio. In other words, they are much thinner than a comparable strength monofilament fishing line.

All this fish-speak aside, shoot for no more than four-pound test fishing line for panfish, maybe even two pound or three pound if you can find it and are not losing too many jigs to structures or poorly-tied knots. I would suggest eight pounds for smaller to medium-size walleye and lines of ten to twenty pounds for larger walleye or pike.

If you are rigging up a tip-up, I suggest purchasing backing line to initially fill the spool and then attaching a section of monofilament line afterwards that is tied to your hook. The advantage of using backing line is that it stays limber in cold weather and has less tendency to coil up on itself and tangle. Since you must pull line in hand over hand when using a tip-up, the backing line offers these two key advantages. However, backing line is a dark, heavy line that is easily visible in the water and should not be tied directly to the hook as it will discourage anything in the vicinity from approaching your bait.

Once the backing line is spooled onto the tip-up, attach approximately five feet of monofilament fishing line in the ten-pound to twenty-pound range to be used as a leader. You can use a lighter monofilament leader of only six pounds if fishing primarily for smaller walleye. My reasoning for suggesting such a short leader is that the working end of the line will get a lot of rough usage and may quickly develop nicks or scrapes that will weaken the line. This short section can easily be changed and maintained with fresh line to help avoid the loss of a fish during your ice fishing adventures. This set-up will provide enough low visibility fishing line in your presentation so as not to spook the fish, will quickly get you into the backing line for easy handling, and will not waste unnecessary amounts of monofilament line.

Connecting Backing Line to a Monofilament Leader

Since there is a significant difference in the diameter of backing line and monofilament line, it makes tying a dependable line-to-line knot a rather difficult task. If you add cold fingers to the mix, the job gets even tougher.

In order to connect the backing and monofilament together, I suggest using a swivel and two separate knots. Using a Palomar knot, tie the backing line directly to the swivel. Using a Trilene knot, tie the monofilament line to the other side of the swivel. Although I am a big fan of the Palomar knot, you can only use this knot when tying something to the end of a line. You could also use a Trilene knot for both the backing line and the monofilament leader, but it pays to know a few knots very well.

Why Knot?

This seems as good a spot as any to discuss how to tie knots. You will either be trying to set up a tip-up from what you just read or getting to the point of tying on the terminal tackle (jigs or hooks), so let's chat about knots.

More knot variations exist than I care to write about, and certainly many more than you care to read about, but knots are a crucial part of any successful fishing. An improperly tied knot will significantly reduce the strength of the line and almost always will rear its ugly head when a large fish is putting your knot to the test. The vast majority of line breaks occur at the knot.

Do not assume that you can just tie a couple of simple overhand knots and that will do the trick. An overhand knot or two is the kiss of death for any of your tackle or fish that you and your children hope to catch. I personally lost an embarrassing number of fish to improperly tied knots as I began my own fishing adventures.

The Palomar and Trilene knots illustrated on the next page are very easy to tie and can quickly be mastered by both you and your children. Both knots can be used for all types of fishing and, when tied properly, will not compromise the strength of your line. They are also great knots for ice fishing since they can be tied in no time at all, keeping the cold weather exposure time of your hands and fingers to a minimum.

The following knot-tying illustrations show the knot being tied directly to a hook. Either knot could be used to tie directly to any terminal tackle or swivel. Although both knots are very easy to tie, please practice each knot before you go fishing. Remember, too, that if all your rods are tied up with gear ready to go at home, you can start your fishing immediately upon arriving at your destination.

When teaching a knot to your child, use a swivel or sinker for them to practice with instead of a hook so you do not risk them getting a poke during their education.

The Trilene Knot

This is a very simple knot and can be tied with these three simple steps:

1. Pull the end of the line through the eye of the swivel or hook twice.

2. Wrap the line around the main line at least five times. Thread the tag end between the eye and coil (loop) of line at the eye of the hook or swivel.

3. Moisten the line and pull the knot tight, trimming the tag end of the line within one-eighth inch of the knot.

> Hint: when tying the Trilene knot, pinch the eye of the swivel or hook between your thumb and forefinger as well as the loop of line at the eye of the knot. This will help hold the loop in place as you wrap the line and hold the loop open, making it much easier to thread the tag end through the loop as you complete the knot.

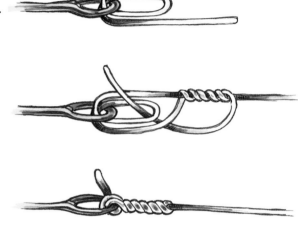

The Trilene Knot

The Palomar Knot

Learning several different knots is a good idea, as different knots serve different needs. This knot is very easy to tie and even a child can quickly become proficient at it with a bit of practice:

1. Double up the fishing line running through the eye of the hook or lure that you intend to tie. You can do this by pushing a loop of line through the eye or by running the line through the eye and then back through in the opposite direction.

2. Tie an overhand knot in the doubled line.

3. Pass the hook through the loop you created; moisten and snug the knot.

4. Trim the tag end within one-eighth inch of the knot.

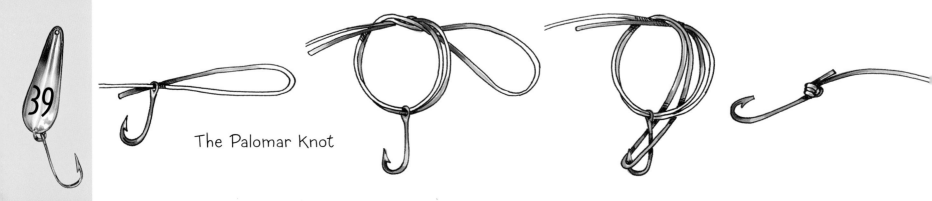

The Palomar Knot

39

Jigs

The most common and favored piece of fishing tackle by the ice fishing population is the jig. While ice fishing, you only have one way to present your offering to the fish and that is a straight vertical direction directly below your feet, hence the value of the jig. Gone is the need for casting or trolling baits that must be horizontally pulled through the water. The exception to this is certain spoons, which act as large-sized jigs and can be effective for larger fish such as walleye, lake trout, or pike.

Plain Jigs

The fishing industry is at its best when it comes to offering a variety of choices in ice fishing jigs. There are countless designs, shapes, and color patterns to entice any and all species of fish that may be the target of ice fishermen. So, as variety is the spice of life, it is also the key element in putting fish on the ice. The general rule of thumb is to use smaller jigs for smaller fish, but you would be surprised at how big a jig some perch will hit. Sunfish and bluegill prefer tiny jigs no bigger than half an inch in length and sometimes as small as a pea. Perch may like these on some days, but on other days prefer a large flashy jig as long as an inch and a half. It pays to carry a variety of jigs and to change your presentation until you find the one they are actively biting the day you happen to be fishing.

Popular colors to include in your jig arsenal are chartreuse, orange, pearl, and black. Jigs come painted in these solid colors, a blend of these colors, or painted on one side and left silver on the other. Most often, they have a black spot or eye painted on them as well.

Jigging Minnows

A very popular summertime lure, the floating Rapala, has a very effective cousin, the jigging Rapala. The jigging Rapala is a weighted Rapala designed specifically for jigging. The jigging Rapala comes in various colors and can be fished plain or baited with a live minnow or minnows on each hook. These baits come in sizes as small as an inch long for perch or crappie and up to three inches long for walleye or lake trout.

Jigging Minnow

My Favorite Jigs: Just Bead It!

My hands-down favorite for panfish are beaded jigs. This just means the jig has a small plastic bead on the hook. The beads may be green, red, or painted with an eye or dot on the bead. The bead acts as bait and also helps prevent the barb of the hook from penetrating the fish's mouth. What does this mean to you? The use of bait on a hook is optional and therefore you can actually catch fish without having to continually re-bait your hook and pull your hands from your toasty warm gloves. Also, by preventing the barb of the hook from penetrating the fish's mouth, you can pull the fish from the water and gently bop it on the ice and, whah lah, the jig will pop free from the fish and again your hands stay in your gloves.

40

You can still use bait on a beaded jig, and sometimes this is preferred given the attitude of the fish. If you are going to use bait, look closely at the beaded jig to make sure the bead does not completely cover the barb of the hook. Without an exposed barb to hold the bait, it will continually slip off as the jig is lowered into the water. While some jigs have the bead glued in place on the hook, others have a moveable bead that can be slid up the hook to expose the barb and enable you to properly bait the hook.

Jigging Spoons

While the intent of this book is to get your children to catch panfish, you may get the urge to try for some larger game such as walleye, pike, or lake trout, and for these species of fish, I suggest larger spoons or jigs. Jigging ice spoons will be of a more narrow design than their open water counterparts. They are generally heavier in nature and many are painted with glow paint for low-light conditions. If you think ice fishing itself is crazy, you would be amazed at the number of ice fishermen who night fish in pursuit of large walleye. Hence, the glow spoons are a great choice. Consistent with jigs, you will find the most popular colors to be chartreuse, orange, black, pearl, silver, or copper. I would suggest chatting with the local tackle shop to determine what the spoon or spoons of choice are in the area you are fishing.

Beaded Jigs

Jigging Spoons

Clips and Swivels

Since a key component to successful jig fishing is changing your offering, you will want to be able to do this as quickly and easily as possible. A regular snap swivel, used in open water fishing, is way too big for this job. Some fly fishermen use a very small clip at the end of their line to change flies, and these same clips are what I suggest you use while ice fishing. You most likely will not find these clips amongst the ice fishing tackle at your local sporting goods store. Take a walk over to the fly fishing department to find these valuable items. Some fly fishing purists may puke at the reference that they would use a clip instead of tying their line directly to their fly, and to those folks I apologize. Simply attach the fly clip to your line using a Palomar or Trilene knot and you can easily change your jigs without having to keep your hands exposed for long periods of time re-tying your line to your jigs.

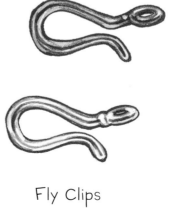

Fly Clips

Swivels

If you will be using larger spoons, I suggest using a very small ball bearing snap swivel. The use of a small snap swivel will improve the action of the spoon and reduce line twist while still enabling you to change spoons without re-tying your line.

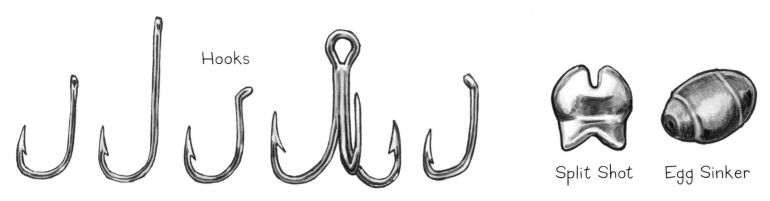

Hooks

Split Shot   Egg Sinker

Hooks and Weights

The only other key pieces of tackle needed are small hooks and split shots for weights. The hooks are primarily used when fishing with minnows, and for this purpose a narrow hook with a longer shank is recommended.

Split shots are lead weights that are pinched onto the fishing line above the hook to aid in lowering your bait in the water. The deeper the water, the heavier split shot(s) you should use.

Last, if you are going to be fishing for larger fish by rod or tip-up, a treble hook works best, but don't use anything that would double as a grappling hook. Treble hooks about the width of a penny are adequate for walleye, with larger trebles more suited for pike.

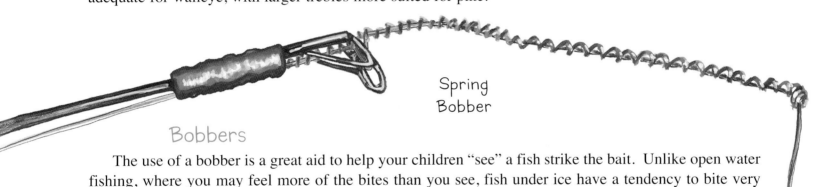

Spring
Bobber

Bobbers

The use of a bobber is a great aid to help your children "see" a fish strike the bait. Unlike open water fishing, where you may feel more of the bites than you see, fish under ice have a tendency to bite very delicately, so much so that you or your child may never feel the take. Even the use of ultra light ice rods may not be enough to readily detect the kissing touch of a modest panfish.

The bobbers that I find best suited for ice fishing are not the floating type that you would be familiar with from open water fishing. The "spring" bobber is my bobber of choice while ice fishing for two reasons. First of all, the spring bobber allows you to fish a variety of depths without having to adjust the bobber. Again, this keeps your hands in your gloves, dry and happy. Second, depending on the style of spring bobber you are using, they are more sensitive than float bobbers and can detect an upward strike that a floating bobber cannot.

My favorite spring bobber is exactly that, a thin, tightly coiled spring about three inches in length that attaches to the end of any ice rod. The fishing line is pulled through the spring and the tackle is attached to the line. This type of spring bobber remains slightly bent over while the bait is in the water. The modest bend in the spring will move up or down as the fish hits and is capable of detecting the slightest bump.

Tip-ups

A tip-up is a contraption used to fish for larger fish that does not have to be constantly tended to like a fishing rod. When set up, it resembles a "t" with a reel at the bottom that holds the fishing line. There is also a spring-loaded flag on the tip-up that pops up when a fish takes the bait. I like the tip-ups with large reels at the bottom to avoid that whole coiling line issue I spoke of previously.

Tip Up Rig

The Bucket

The single most universal and crucial piece of equipment is the under-appreciated pickle bucket or five-gallon bucket. This one simple device serves as a rod holder, tackle box, food cooler, fish cooler, general storage locker, and last but not least, a fishing stool.

You can purchase tricked out versions of "the bucket" at your local sporting goods store that come with a padded seat, a swivel seat, a padded swivel seat, tackle compartment, canvas outside pockets, and so on. However, many restaurants will be happy to provide you with a free one should you use your manners and politely ask for one, not forgetting to say "please."

Once you have obtained "the bucket" and accompanying lid, you can easily modify this item by popping off the lid and cutting about half of it off. Replace the lid and you now have an opening in which to place your rods on your trek out onto the ice. There is your rod holder.

While you are fishing, you will most likely be squatting on "the bucket." That same opening, when placed between your legs, can be used to toss your fish into instead of laying them on the ice and advertising your catch to other fishermen. There is your fish cooler.

You could cut a thin piece of plywood into an eleven-by-fourteen-inch rectangle and slide the wood, lengthwise, into the middle of the bucket. Now you have a dual compartment bucket, one for fish and one for rods or extra clothes such as gloves. There is your general storage fish-cooler-combo bucket.

If you are not a do-it-yourselfer, you can purchase a molded seat/compartment that fits into any pickle bucket. This handy item will provide a cushioned flip-up seat and a compartment for your miscellaneous tackle items.

Let's not forget that you are going to have kids with you and "the bucket" makes for very inexpensive seating for each of them. As well, they can each carry their own snack or beverage of choice, typically hot chocolate, in their bucket with them. Thus, "the bucket" becomes the food cooler.

One last suggestion: since fish tend to have a little personal odor issue, lining your bucket with a plastic bag before heading out allows you to easily and cleanly remove your day's catch upon your return home.

43

Food and Whine

Well, not necessarily in this order. If you are bringing kids, you must bring food and something to drink. The drink part is easy, since nothing is more loved by kids in the winter than hot chocolate. A word to the wise: do not put marshmallows in the thermos as they will become a permanent part of the thermos. A thermos of hot coffee for yourself is an added treat.

The thermos is truly an amazing invention. It keeps hot stuff hot and cold stuff cold, never mixing up the two. It has never made my hot stuff cold or my cold stuff hot. How does it know? Okay, it's a joke!

The food thing is up to you, but be mindful of foods that are easily susceptible to freezing. Cookies, donuts, or granola bars make a great snack and each is improved when dipped in hot chocolate or coffee.

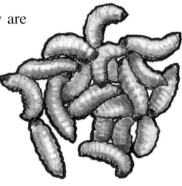
Spike

I like to take a purposeful break for hot chocolate and snack time. It gets our minds off the fishing for a little bit and acts as a nice distraction if the fishing is slow. Plus, I like to eat as much as my kids and taking a break with them is just as enjoyable for me.

Bait

Winter is not the time or the place for cute, wriggly nightcrawlers or garden worms. Say hello to the disgusting and disrespected maggot, known by kinder terms as a "spike" to ice fishermen. You can actually buy them in winter at any bait store.

I bet you didn't know that some maggots have tails and are referred to as "mousies" as they resemble a tiny little mouse. Mousies are also a very effective ice fishing bait.

Mousies

Wax worms are a much larger version of this bait, tails not included, though they are not waxy at all.

Wigglers are mayfly larvae that are about the ugliest bait you can use while ice fishing.

Spikes, mousies, and wax worms have a relatively tough skin that oftentimes allows you to catch multiple fish on one bait before it is eventually yanked off the hook. All of these are purchased in small plastic containers that are packed with sawdust so you can keep your hands dry when fishing with them.

Wax Worms

When using spikes, mousies, or wax worms, simply run the hook through their body, closer to one end of the bait, to allow much of the bait to stick out from the hook.

Wigglers, on the other hand, are packed in the same style container but must be kept in water to stay alive. This is a slightly wet-handed bait

Wiggler

to use. Wigglers have a very soft exoskeleton and are not very durable on the hook but panfish, especially perch, love them.

When using wigglers, you run the hook through the main part of the body, leaving the tail to slowly move back and forth. If you are using very small wigglers, you may have to place more than one on the hook to get the attention of the fish. If you are constantly getting robbed of your wigglers, try sewing the hook through the body by running the hook lengthwise from the head and pushing it all the way through the tail. This method should leave little opportunity for the fish to continue stealing your bait.

Any of these baits will last for some time in your refrigerator should you have leftovers at the end of your outing. Please keep in mind that since most of these baits are fly larvae, should you leave anything but the wigglers in your pocket and store them at room temperature, you will eventually end up with a container full of flies.

Though minnows are the coldest bait you will use while ice fishing because they involve getting your hands wet each time you bait the hook, they, too, have their place among ice fishing baits and at times may be the only bait fish are interested in. Minnow fishing with a bobber can be a great way to introduce kids to ice fishing as they do not have to jig the rod to enhance the presentation; they simply hold the rod still while the minnow swims around and does the attracting for them.

Minnows should be hooked through the lips or through the body, just behind the dorsal fin. When hooking a minnow through the lips, run the hook up from the bottom of the minnow through the lips and out the top of the head. If you run the hook too close to the edge of the lips, the minnow will tear right off your hook. If you run the hook too far back in the head, you will go through the brain and there goes your lively minnow.

Lip
Hook

When hooking a minnow near the dorsal fin, the center fin on top of a fish's back, place the hook midway between the dorsal and tail fin. Note the line that runs along the side of the minnow, from head to tail. Place the hook just above this line to avoid running the hook through the spine of the fish and putting an end to its swimming.

Dorsal
Fin Hook

An old but effective trick that fishermen still use today is to clip a portion of the tail fin on a minnow so that the minnow swims even harder to move around. The additional movement of the minnow aids in attracting fish.

Electronics

Where would we be today without the infusion of electronics to kick things up a notch? In an effort to keep this sport as affordable as possible, I will touch on just a few items that are available to enhance your ice fishing adventure.

If you don't want to drill open numerous holes looking for the drop-off or deeper water, you can

purchase a hand-held depth sounder that resembles a "D" cell flashlight that when held to the ice offers up a digital display of the depth.

From here, you can get fish finders and/or flashers that provide information including depth, fish location, structure, and even offer GPS capabilities.

Finally, if you just can't get your child to do anything without involving a video screen, the underwater camera is the key to getting your child out fishing with you. This is a video camera that will show you and your children what is going on below your feet. The camera will provide a great education as to how fish react to your bait and your jigging presentation. It can also entertain beyond its effectiveness as fishermen get so caught up watching the fish that they miss setting the hook when the fish finally bites the bait.

Ice Spud or Auger

The ice spud, a steel pole with a chiseled business end, is essential for early-season ice fishing so that you can test the ice as you walk by striking the ice in front of you. This item can be purchased with a smooth chiseled end or with a toothed chiseled end. The toothed model chips through ice much quicker than the smooth-ended spud and will greatly reduce your workload in punching open holes. As the season progresses and the ice thickens beyond six inches, it becomes a very strenuous task to chip open a hole with a spud. This will greatly limit your desire to move around on the ice and fish different spots due to the exertion involved in spudding open new holes.

In any season, the auger is a much more efficient tool for cutting open holes in the ice. The auger requires less effort and cuts open a much neater hole, preventing the loss of a fish by catching the fishing line on a jagged edge made by a spud. The manual auger is offered in many diameters, but stick to the size necessary for the task at hand. If you're only going to be fishing for panfish, the smaller diameter auger is lighter to carry and drills through the ice more easily and quickly than a large auger. If you really get into it, nothing beats a motorized power auger for cutting through late-season ice that can measure up to two feet or better.

Auger

Ice Spud

Ice Scoop

The first thing you need in ice fishing is something to punch a hole in the ice. The second thing you need is something to remove all the ice chips from your fishing hole. The ice scoop is really just a large perforated ladle that drains the water as you skim the ice chips from the hole. Ice scoops are very inexpensive and you may want to buy extras. Children love to scoop the chips from the hole and fling them in the air or slide them across the ice. These same children are also proficient at dropping things at very inopportune times. Bring just one scoop and it will almost surely find its way to the bottom of the lake.

Ice Scoop

Ice Soccer

This section has nothing to do with equipment or how to ice fish, but since we are talking about cutting ice holes (watch how you say this), it applies. If you are on new ice without a snow cover, try to

46

chip large chunks of ice from the hole. These ice chunks will slide endlessly across the ice and provide lots of fun for kids to play around with. They may have a game of ice soccer while ice fishing, and as long as they're happy, it adds to everyone's enjoyment. As always, use caution not to slide the ice chunk over untested ice, and always test the area where your children will be playing to be sure the ice is safe.

Gaff

Gaff

A gaff is really just a huge hook attached to a handle, normally about two to three feet in length, that is used to land large fish. In the summer, we use a net to land fish that are too large to be lifted from the water as the fishing line would break. In the winter, we cannot fit a net into the hole so we use a gaff. Once a large fish is played out, the fisherman pulls its head to the surface of the water and inserts the gaff into the fish at the bottom of the mouth. The fish is then lifted from the water with the gaff.

Sled

One thing all ice fishermen have in common is only two arms. Therefore, they are limited in how much they can single-handedly carry out onto the ice. Enter the plastic sled. I suggest using a plastic utility sled with raised sides and an overhanging lip around the edge. You can place "the bucket" or "buckets" in the sled and bungee cord them down should it be windy or bumpy on the ice. Also, the sled can be used as a child transport device so that you can access more ice without exhausting your kids, just yourself. Most importantly, should you have a successful outing and fill a bucket with fish, the walk back in will be much more enjoyable as you pull your catch back across the ice instead of lugging it in your arms along with all your other gear.

Ice
Sled

Ice Shanty

The ice shanty can really make ice fishing much more enjoyable for everyone. Just the fact that you have the ability to break the wind (not that kind!) is so important to keeping everyone warm. You can bring a heater, but on most days, just the body heat of those inside will allow you to fish with your coat and gloves off. The ice shanty can also double as a sled, since many portable shanties have a black plastic sled bottom as their base with a fold-over or pop-up canvas structure affixed to the sled.

The coolest thing a shanty does is accentuate the light exuding from the ice, thus allowing you to see into the water and oftentimes watch the fishing action without the addition of an expensive underwater camera. Depending on the depth and clarity of the water, it can be like looking into an aquarium, which will entertain you and your children for hours on end. The best underwater visibility is achieved when the shanty is dark inside, by sealing all the doors and windows.

Shanty Set-Up

When setting up a shanty, first clear the area of any snow with a small shovel or just by sliding your boots sideways along the ice. Open the shanty floor and slide it onto the area you have cleared. There will be holes in the shanty floor to access the ice. Make a mark on the ice in each opening where you'd like a hole, slide the shanty aside, and cut your holes. Remove the ice chips and set them off to the side (as you would onions in a recipe) for use later. Slide the shanty back over the holes and pack the bottom of the shanty with the ice chips and snow to keep out wind and light. On a very windy day, it will be vital to pack the shanty base with snow to prevent the shanty from blowing across the ice as soon as you step out of it.

Ice
Shanty

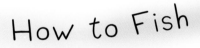

How to Fish

Dead Sticking/Still Fishing

No false advertising here! Simply keep the stick (pole) dead so it doesn't move. That's the whole secret to this method of fishing. Fish seem to move slower and be more methodical in cold water. They may stop and analyze a bait for some time before deciding to bite it or not. When they are in this mood, even the slightest twitch of the rod will spook them away.

This is the easiest method to use with your children as no discipline is required. The rods can be set in rod holders and simply watched by your children.

When using this type of set-up, lower the bait to the bottom and then reel in six to twelve inches of line so that you keep the bait just off the bottom. Vary how far off the bottom you present your bait until you come into fish.

I recommend using live bait when dead sticking as something needs to attract the fish to the hook.

48

If you're not moving the bait yourself, the sight and smell of live bait will be your attractant. Live minnows work best, hooked just behind the dorsal fin or through the lips (see illustrations on page 45). Either method will keep the minnow lively and swimming happily in the water. Wigglers are another awesome bait to use in this method of fishing. There are many days when you will catch more fish on wigglers than on any other bait or all others combined. After that, you can try mousies, spikes, or wax worms, but you may want to use a smaller hook when you switch to these forms of bait.

For this type of fishing, I suggest adding a very light spring bobber to the end of the fishing rod. The spring bobber will bend slightly under the weight of the sinker and bait and this is key as fish may bite down, further bending the spring or taking the bait so lightly that the weight is relieved and the spring bobber becomes straight. Either way, any movement up or down indicates a fish is biting your bait.

A Typical
Dead Stick Set-Up

Under ordinary circumstances I recommend having your child pull up on the rod as soon as the fish hits to set the hook and bring the fish in, but winter fish can be fussy and may be tough to hook until they really take the bait in their mouths. If your son or daughter sets the hook at the first bite and hooks the fish consistently, have them keep it up. If they're missing fish, have them wait until the fish really takes the bait before setting the hook. This part may take some discipline on the part of you and your child.

In letting the fish take the bait, the spring bobber and maybe even the rod tip will bounce up and down just slightly as the fish begins to hit. Once the fish takes the bait into its mouth, the rod will bend aggressively toward the hole, and that's the time to set the hook and reel the fish up.

Jigging Action: Do a Little Jig!

Jigging is one of the most effective methods of ice fishing. Whether you are fishing for finicky bluegill or trophy walleye, learning how to properly jig will put these fish on ice. Jigging does not have to be complicated, and children can use this method by simply moving their rods up and down, further developing their own style of jigging as they grow older.

There is no special way to rig a jig to your fishing line; it is simply tied or clipped to the end of the fishing line. Again, I suggest using a small fly snap when jigging with small jigs and a small snap swivel for larger jigs so that you can quickly change jigs without retying the line.

The depth you should concentrate on is typically the waters within one foot of the bottom. To find this zone, drop the line down until the bait hits bottom. You can tell you've reached bottom when the line goes slack. With the rod tip near the hole, reel in the slack in the line. Now you will know that when the rod tip is lowered at the end of a downward jig, your bait will be at the bottom.

49

Just what is proper jigging, you ask? The proper jigging technique all depends on the species you are fishing for, the water you are fishing, the alignment of the sun to the moon, and many other factors. As well, the same jigging rhythm may not be successful each time you're out fishing. It is very important to vary your jigging pattern until you find the reaction from the fish that you are looking for: an active bite.

The action of jigging is much more than just raising and lowering your arm. You can try long jigs by raising and lowering your arm a few feet at a time, quicker short-up-and-down jigs, quick-on-the-up and slow-on-the-down jigs, and quick-on-the-down and slow-on-the-up jigs. Jigging also does not have to be just up and down; you can make circles with the rod or just shake the rod a bit to get the jig to vibrate. Any of these actions can work on any given ice fishing adventure. Heck, have your kids do the hokey pokey with the rod, because in ice fishing, getting your jig to dance properly is what it's all about.

Don't forget to pause occasionally during your jigging presentation. Oftentimes, though fish are attracted by the jigging, they will not strike the jig until it comes to a complete stop. Sometimes it takes a minute or two of being still in between jigs to settle the fish down and get them to strike.

Although jigging can be an effective way to fish, it can require patience and discipline to fish in this manner and it may have to wait until your children are older. But all kids are different, and while some may be content to let a rod sit and just watch a bobber, another may enjoy the challenge of finding the right action that gets the fish biting. Once a child starts catching fish on a jig, all the kids will want one, believe me!

Matching the Rig or the Jig to the Fish

Bluegill

Bluegill have very small mouths and are among the most finicky cold water fish to put in the bucket. Many ice fishermen swear that if you can successfully master the art of jigging for bluegill, you can successfully jig for just about anything. I suggest a very small teardrop jig in chartreuse, orange, red/white, or pearl/orange. Lace the jig with a spike or mousie for bait and try short subtle strokes with your jigging presentation. Be very patient and very still in between jigs, as gills like to hit during the downtime between jigs. I also suggest attaching a spring bobber to your rod to detect extremely subtle hits from the bluegill. Bluegill are notorious for biting so lightly in the winter that many fishermen never feel their bite and therefore never land them. A lightweight spring bobber will react to the slightest kiss by a fish and will help you and your kids put some gills in the bucket.

Perch

The old standby I like best is a beaded jig tipped with a mousie or spike. I prefer to quickly raise and lower the rod tip, letting the jig free-fall and dart wildly on its way back down. Many beaded jigs are barbless or hide the barb with the bead. This can make it difficult to get bait to stay on, but by the same token, once the fish start to hit in numbers, they fall right off your hook onto the ice and you can quickly get back to fishing. Even better, you may not need any bait at all with a beaded jig, as simply the action of the jig alone and the bead, which looks like something appetizing to a fish, provides plenty of action. I like using this presentation best in shallow water of less than fifteen feet.

50

Perch Spreader Rig

This is a rig that works well when fishing in deep water. Although you can buy pre-made spreader rigs, you can easily set them up for a fraction of the cost. You will need two small pre-tied hooks and a small sinker. Attach the sinker to the end of the fishing line by using a small snap swivel or by tying it directly to the line. Then add the hooks directly to the line about one foot and two feet up from the sinker.

Pre-tied hooks have about a six-inch length of line attached to them with a loop at the end of the line. Run the hook through the loop around the main fishing line and pull the hook until the new loop you just created tightens around the main line. You can also vary the distance between hooks as well as the baits on each hook.

Walleye

When jigging for walleye, you will have to move from your smaller ice jigs to much larger lead head jigs or spoons. I prefer to use spoons tipped with a large minnow when fishing for walleye. Most spoons will have a treble (three-pointed) hook attached. You can hook one large minnow to one of the hooks or try hooking a small minnow to each of the three hooks to give the appearance of a small

Perch Spreader Rig

school of minnows moving through the water. When hooking minnows to any walleye jig, place the hook through the lips of the minnow to keep it as lively and natural-looking as possible.

I like to use a jigging pattern with a steady up and down jig rhythm, lifting the jig up about one foot off the bottom and slowly lowering the jig back to the bottom so as not to allow any slack in the line. Walleye seem to prefer hitting the jig on their way down and you can get a better hook set by keeping the line tight as you lower your rod. However, it sometimes pays to bang the jig off the bottom by raising your rod and quickly lowering it so that the jig free-falls to the bottom. When the jig hits the bottom, it will kick up dirt or sand and give the walleye the impression that something is alive and active at the bottom that probably tastes pretty good, too.

Walleye are a much larger fish than perch or bluegill and will feel noticeably heavier when hooked on a light ice rod. Your child may freak out initially at the weight of a large fish on an ice rod. Just encourage your child to hold on tightly to the rod and enjoy the battle of getting the fish on top of the ice.

Thumbs Up for Tip-Ups

What on earth is a tip-up, you ask? In simple form, it is two pieces of wood in a t-shaped pattern with a spool of fishing line attached to the bottom of the "t." Attached to the top of the "t" is a flag on a length of metal band that bends down to a release. The release is triggered when a fish pulls line off the spool, sending the flag up and indicating that a fish is biting the line. The tip-up rests in the ice fishing hole and is removed once the flag goes up. There is no reel attached to the tip-up, so the line is brought in by hand, end over end. The tip-up sits in a hole on its own and you do not fish another line through the same hole that has a tip-up in it.

I love fishing with tip-ups. Tip-ups allow you to have an extra line in the water and cover greater areas than you could with just one pole in a hole at a time. Also, tip-ups are most commonly used for larger species of fish so when the flag goes up, you know you have hooked a larger fish and the fun is just beginning!

To keep everything legal, a tip-up counts as a line in the water, though it is not connected to a fishing rod. Every state has a limit of lines in the water per fisherman, and most commonly it is two lines per person. It would be legal to have your child fish with a rod and have a tip-up set up in the same vicinity. Most states also require that your name be affixed to the tip-up so that the DNR or MNR can see to whom it belongs if out on patrol. I suggest reading your state's fishing regulations as they relate to ice fishing and the use of tip-ups to stay within the legal boundaries.

The best place to use a tip-up is in areas where there is a good potential for large fish. If your goal is simply to go perch fishing or bluegill fishing to put some food on the plate, you may not want to bother with tip-ups. The purpose of fishing with a tip-up is to catch larger fish. If you set up tip-ups in the immediate area where you are panfishing, the larger fish that are attracted by your tip-up will drive away the smaller ones that you are fishing for with your ice rod. However, if you are out in deeper water fishing for perch and there is a shallow weedbed nearby, set out some tip-ups near the weedbed for pike and then move out into the deeper water for the perch. This way you can maximize your fishing opportunities.

When purchasing a tip-up, like so many other products you buy, the line is sold separately. Since a tip-up line is retrieved hand over hand, it is preferable to line the spool with an inexpensive backing line and then just use five feet of monofilament as a leader. The backing line resists coiling and stays soft in the cold weather, making it easier to handle than monofilament line. Connecting the lines can be done in one of two ways, either by tying the leader directly to the backing line using a line-to-line knot or by tying a small swivel to the backing using a Palomar knot and then tying the monofilament to the other end of the swivel using a Trilene knot. Line-to-line knots can be difficult to master and are even harder with cold fingers. That is why I like to just use a swivel and a couple of simple knots to do the job.

Tip Up Rig

The rigging of a tip-up is very simple. A weight is needed to get your bait down in the water, normally within ten to twelve inches of the hook. I like to use an egg sinker and a split shot for the weight. The line feeds through the egg sinker and then a split shot can be pinched on the line below the egg sinker to keep the sinker from sliding down to the hook.

For the hook, use a very sharp treble hook. Since large fish have tougher bone structure in their mouths, hooks must be very sharp to do the job right. For walleye, initially lower the bait within one foot of the bottom, but then vary the depth in small increments if there is no fish activity. For pike, whose eyes are on top of their head, the bait must be presented at a depth which is a bit higher than where you expect the fish to be swimming.

Tip-ups are almost exclusively baited with large minnows. For walleye, I prefer blue minnows. Good-sized blue minnows will be two to three inches in length and the use of a smaller treble hook will enable them to still swim naturally. For pike, much larger bait is used such as chubs or shiners that measure six to ten inches in length and a large-sized treble hook. Regardless of the bait you are using, hook the minnow through the back, just behind the dorsal fin, with one of the hooks from the treble. Be careful not to place the hook too deeply below the back so that you avoid hitting the spine in the fish which will paralyze your bait and leave the fish lifeless in the water. Make sure you bring the hook through the fish so that the barb of the hook passes all the way through the bait fish. If not, the fish will swim off your hook and your flag will never fly.

There Goes the Flag!

The best part of fishing with a tip-up is seeing the flag go flying. This means that a big fish has hit your bait. Don't freak! This is fun, fun, fun! What you need to do is set the hook and pull the fish in by retrieving the line hand over hand. Here is the best way to accomplish this task: when you get to your tip-up, look at the spool, which is just underwater, to see if line is still being pulled from it. The fish may have hit and still be running with the bait in its mouth, or it may have stopped to swallow the bait. If the fish is still running out line, wait until it stops to remove the tip-up from the hole.

To involve your children in this excitement, pull the tip-up from the hole and hand it to your child, having him hold it the same way it was sitting in the hole with the spool facing down. Grab onto the line and gently pull the line until it is taut with the fish. Immediately at this point, give the line a good solid tug to set the hook in the fish's mouth. Feeling the sting of the hook, the fish may run again. This is why it is important to hold the tip-up the same way it was positioned when sitting on the ice so that the line can pull from the spool if necessary and not get tangled in the tip-up.

Pike have a tendency to hit the bait, run a short time, stop to swallow the bait, and then proceed to run off again. Although it requires patience, wait for the second run before you set the hook. Many times with pike, if you set the hook on the initial run, you will just pull the bait from their mouths.

As you bring in line on the fish, do not worry about winding it on the spool. Just pile it neatly on the ice. If the fish runs while being pulled in, continue to hold the line in your hands and let the line slip through your fingers, keeping a slight tension on the line. Try not to let the line go slack, as this can cause the hook to free itself from the fish. When the fish stops running, continue to pull line in on the fish and do not allow it to rest. If the fish feels very heavy, do not try to rush the fight and horse the fish in. Be patient by keeping steady pressure on the line or allowing the fish to pull line through your fingers when taking off on a run.

Once the fish tires, bring its head through the hole and lift it just out of the water. Immediately grab the fish from below the gills or behind the head, squeeze firmly, and pull it from the water. If you have a gaff, hook the gaff in the bottom of the jaw and remove the fish from the water by lifting it with the gaff. If you have hooked a small fish, you can pull it right up out of the water with the line, but if it is anything of size, use your hand or a gaff to land it.

Next comes one of the most important steps. Once the fish is out of the water and lying on the ice, have your child set down the tip-up and raise his or her arms high in the air. Then commence to give a

53

barrage of high fives and whoopees! Do not skip this step!

Preserving the Memory

One of the best things that fishing provides is warm wonderful memories, even from ice fishing. There is just no better way to relive those memories than with pictures from the adventure. The key to great pictures is taking them at the height of your children's emotion, and that time is when they have just caught a fish. There is something so cool and exhilarating about catching a fish, and it shows itself in tremendous expression on your child's face. Snap a few shots of your children fishing as well as when they have landed their fish. These photos truly will be priceless.

Fresh fish are not only good for eating, but that's when they are most photogenic as well. Snap your photos right when the fish have been caught, as this is when the fish are most colorful. Pictures shot later upon your return home will render colorless, lifeless fish and typically children too pooped from adventure to push out the same great smiles they gave you while on their excursion.

Fishing Journal

Okay, well maybe I lied: the other great way to preserve the memory of your fishing adventures is to keep a fishing journal. Record the people involved, the place you fished, the weather, the tackle used, and the catch, even if there was no catch. The journal will not only help bring past adventures to life, it will be a great education as to what worked or did not work last time out and where you were when you caught fish. I have come to realize this thing called age blurs the memory, but the journal keeps it clear for years to come.

It is also a good idea to have your children keep their own fishing journals if they are of writing age. The fishing journal will not only promote their writing skills, it will also provide the same story in their own perspective – a perspective that may surprise and entertain you. If your kids are not of writing age, ask for their input as to what was important enough on your adventure to be included in the fishing journal.

How to Clean Fish

Now that you have a nice batch of fish, what do you do with them? First of all, if you are going to keep fish for a meal, avoid leaving them on the ice as you catch them and instead place them in your bucket. This will help slow the fish from freezing prior to your return home so you won't have to thaw them in order to clean them.

That being said, where is the best place to clean your fish? Naturally, your buddy's house is the best place, but if you must clean them on home turf, be mindful of your spouse and her uncanny ability to smell fish in the area that you cleaned them for at least one month following your actions.

Get yourself a good cleaning board, preferably one that can be dedicated to future fish cleanings and not your best everyday cutting board. Next, you will need a very sharp, thin-bladed knife and here I cannot stress the "very" enough. Most common household knives are not up to the task of cleaning fish as the blades are too thick and they just are not sharp enough. My favorite filet knife is manufactured by Rapala. The knives come in varying lengths based on the task at hand, are very sharp from the factory, and can be brought back to original sharpness with ease. The latest rage in fish cleaning is electric filet knives that speed the process significantly. This will make a nice addition as you grow proficient in bringing home fish for dinner.

Good preparation can make this process quick and easy. Line a garbage can with a plastic bag for fish entrails and never place them directly into a garbage can as the clean-up is endless. Assuming you may be cleaning your fish on a kitchen counter or workbench, cover the work area with newspaper as you may have some "spill" on the counter as you clean your fish.

A word of warning before you start cleaning fish: your fingers will get very cold or perhaps even numb from cleaning nearly frozen fish. Be very mindful of the blade at all times throughout the filleting process. It is very easy to get a painfully deep cut and not realize it until your fingertips begin to thaw.

The following fish-cleaning process will quickly yield skinless, boneless filets of meat without the time-consuming and extremely messy task of scaling the fish. This is one of the easiest ways to clean fish, especially panfish such as perch or bluegill:

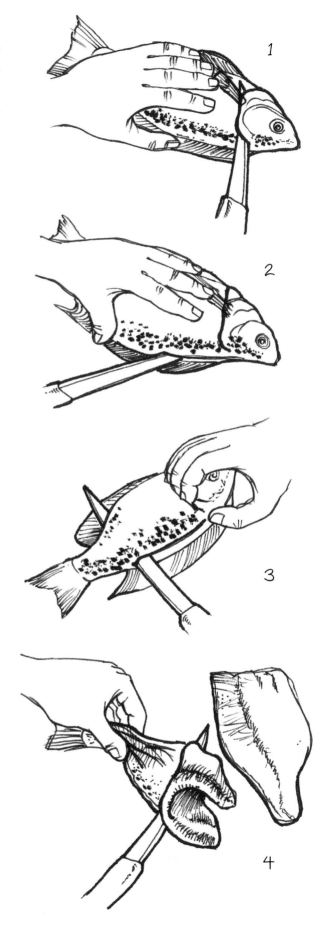

55

1. Place the fish on the cleaning board with the top of the fish facing you and the belly of the fish facing away from you. Place the blade of the knife directly behind the gill and the pectoral fin, cutting straight down toward the board until you hit the backbone of the fish. Be careful not to exert too much pressure on the downward cut as you can easily slice through the backbone making it a real challenge to continue filleting the fish.

2. Turn the blade towards the tail of the fish and slide it along the backbone, passing through the entire fish. During this cut, you will be slicing through the rib cage of the fish. If your knife is sharp enough, push your way right through the ribs and gently through to the tail. Otherwise, a slight sawing action will help you easily get through the fish.

3. Complete the cut at the tail of the fish, which will result in removing the filet from the body of the fish. Flip the fish over to its other side and repeat steps one and two.

4. Place the filets, skin side down, and place the knife blade at the tail between the meat of the filet and the skin, keeping the blade parallel to the cutting board. Push the knife completely through the filet and this will neatly remove the skin from the fish, without the hassle of scaling the filet. At this point, you will have a skinless filet, but the rib cage will still be attached. Simply slide the point of the blade around the rib cage, within the filet, to remove the rib bones.

Storing Fish

If you will not be consuming the fish in the next few days, you can safely store fish in the freezer for months without the taste or quality deteriorating. The key to properly freezing fish is to avoid air coming into contact with the filets. You can accomplish this by vacuum packing the fish, but you will need to have a vacuum packer on hand and the necessary packing material. The other way is to place the filets in a Ziplock freezer bag and fill the bag with water until the filets are covered. Seal the bag, while pressing out all the air left in the bag. This method of freezing will also keep the fish as fresh as possible while not exposing the filets to freezer burn.

It is a good idea to label and date the bags or packages of fish before filling them with the filets. Also, fill the bags with just enough filets for one meal so that you can get several meals out of your catch and not waste the filets for which you have worked so hard.

Cooking Fish

More and more, health advocates are promoting the inclusion of fish in our diets. Fish provide a very healthy alternative with valuable vitamins that we may not be getting in the foods that make up our routine daily diets. Then there is the old adage that fish is brain food, but since we caught these fish while out ice fishing, you can toss that idea to the curb!

Keep in mind that fish starts off as a healthy meal but can easily be compromised by the process in which we cook the fish. An inch of batter, bacon grease, and a vat of tartar sauce does nothing to add to the health status of fresh-caught fish. Also, since our fish are so fresh, there should be no fishy smell or taste that we have to try to cover up.

56

Recipes

On this page are a couple of methods of cooking that our family enjoys when we have the luxury of fresh-caught perch to be prepared. Both recipes use just one pound of perch filets, but who are we kidding? Perch is among the most desired fish for table fare and you may need a pound of filets per person. Simply adjust the recipe accordingly and enjoy your fresh-caught meal.

Pan-Fried Perch with Hint of Garlic

(serves two to four fisherpeople)

Ingredients

1 pound of perch filets

1 cup flour

1/8 teaspoon garlic powder
(use more or less to your liking)

Dash of salt

1/2 teaspoon dried parsley (or finely chopped fresh parsley)

2 large eggs

1/2 cup olive oil, corn oil, or sunflower oil for cooking

1. Mix flour, garlic powder, salt, and parsley together in a large shallow bowl. (You should be able to taste the garlic in the mixture by testing with a finger poke and quick lick.)

2. Scramble the eggs in a separate bowl. In the cooking industry, this is known as an egg wash.

3. Rinse and pat the filets dry with a paper towel prior to cooking.

4. Heat cooking oil.

5. Dip the filets into the scrambled eggs.

6. Dip the filets into the flour mixture.

7. Place filets in pan and cook until golden brown. Flip over filets and cook until other side is golden brown. For the average-sized fish, this should take no longer than a couple of minutes per side in a hot skillet.

8. To test if fish is done, the filet should easily pull apart and appear to be bright white all the way through. If the fish is not cooked thoroughly, the filet will not easily break apart and will appear translucent.

9. Enjoy while hot!

The following recipe comes from my father, a tremendous cook and a passionate fan of using homemade Italian breadcrumbs on just about anything.

First, the breadcrumb recipe, which is more than you will need for just one fish dinner but can be used on anything from fish to chicken to chops. Unused breadcrumbs can be stored in a freezer for several months.

Anthony's Sicilian Breadcrumbs

4 cups coarsely ground breadcrumbs
 (yes, hard old Italian bread when crushed is perfect)

1½ cups finely chopped Italian parsley

1 cup grated Romano cheese

1 level tablespoon ground pepper

Perch ala Anthony

(serves two to four fisherpeople)

1 pound of perch filets (rinse and pat dry filets prior to cooking)

1 cup of Anthony's Sicilian Breadcrumbs

2 large eggs

1/4 teaspoon salt or Chef Paul Prudhomme's Seafood Magic (a seasoning)

1/2 cup corn oil

1. Place just the amount of breadcrumbs you wish to use into a large shallow bowl.

2. Scramble eggs in separate bowl and add salt or Prudhomme's Seafood Magic.

3. Dip fish filets into scrambled eggs and lay in seasoned breadcrumbs on both sides. Breadcrumbs will stick to filets.

4. Heat corn oil in a large frying pan on a low to medium setting.

5. Sauté filets for two or three minutes per side, depending on thickness of fish and until breadcrumbs are golden brown.

6. Serve hot and enjoy!

The breadcrumbs or flour coating may absorb a fair amount of the cooking oil throughout the frying process. If the pan is running out of oil while you are cooking, add additional oil, bring back to temperature, and continue cooking.

NAME THAT FISH!
Family Game

NAME THAT FISH! is a fun game designed to help children identify the various species of popular fresh-water game fish and learn about their preferred habitats, diets, and baits of choice. This is a great game to be played in between bites while fishing or as an enticer between much-anticipated fishing adventures.

To play, first read the clues for each fish to your children and point out the identifying clues as illustrated in the picture of each fish. Then read back the clues to your children (naturally with them not looking at the pictures) and see how many clues it takes before they can **NAME THAT FISH!**

Once they have been through the game a few times, pick a fish and ask your children how many clues they can recite back to you from memory. You will be surprised at how quickly they catch on and will be able to identify their fish.

58

BLUEGILL

My name is how you know me.

My Munchies

Spikes   Mousies

My Hangouts

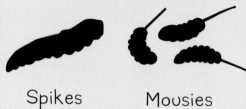

Weedy   Sticky   Ponds
Beds   Piles

The Biggest Ever

4 POUNDS

1/3 POUND

········ Average Size

How to Catch Me!

A very small Teardrop jig baited with a spike or mousie and jigged very slowly can turn on finicky winter bluegills. Bluegill can bite very lightly so pay attention to your rod tip or even movement in your fishing line.

Short body that is very narrow near tail

Light green color, faded stripes from top to bottom

Tail is slightly forked

Blue spot on tip of gill, orange patch below chin

59

ROCKBASS

My name is where you will find me.

My Munchies

Mousies   Spikes

Small Minnows

My Hangouts

Rocky   Weedy   Sticky
Bottoms   Beds   Piles

The Biggest Ever

3 POUNDS

1/3 POUND ······ Average Size

How to Catch Me!

A small jig baited with a minnow and fished above rocky piles or weedy beds is a sure bet. A small plain hook tipped with a small minnow can also work well.

Many rows of small black dots from head to tail

Dark patches across the side

Dark spot on gill

Greenish brown body

60

CRAPPIE

Just a fish, not a bad word.

My Munchies

Small Minnows

My Hangouts

Weedy Beds   Sunken Logs   Sticky Piles

The Biggest Ever

5 POUNDS

1/3 POUND ·····Average Size

How to Catch Me!

A small jig or plain hook baited with a small minnow and fished near the bottom works best. Crappies tend to be active in late afternoon hours or even early evening.

Short body with narrow tail, little forking

Small head but bigger mouth than bluegill

Dark patches or stripes on body and fins

Greenish brown or yellowish brown body

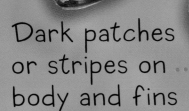

61

NORTHERN PIKE

Long, toothy, and slimy is what I am all about.

My Munchies

Large Minnows

Chubs   Shiners

My Hangouts

Weedy   Lily   Sunken
Beds   Pads   Logs

The Biggest Ever

46 POUNDS

4 POUNDS   Average Size

How to Catch Me!

A tip-up baited with a large minnow, chub, or shiner and fished near a weedy bed, sticky pile, or other structure consistently catches pike. A dead stick baited with a large minnow can also work well.

Fin on back located near tail fin

Long skinny body

Big sharp teeth

Greenish body with white spots

Fins tipped with orange

WALLEYE

Big eyes help me see well at night.

My Munchies

Minnows

My Hangouts

Rocky Bottoms | Gravelly Bottoms | Weedy Beds

The Biggest Ever

20 POUNDS

2 POUNDS

Average Size

How to Catch Me!

A dead stick baited with a blue minnow, fished within one to three feet off of the bottom, is very effective. This same presentation could be used with a tip-up. Jigging a spoon or a jigging minnow baited with a blue minnow or several small minnows near the bottom works well, too.

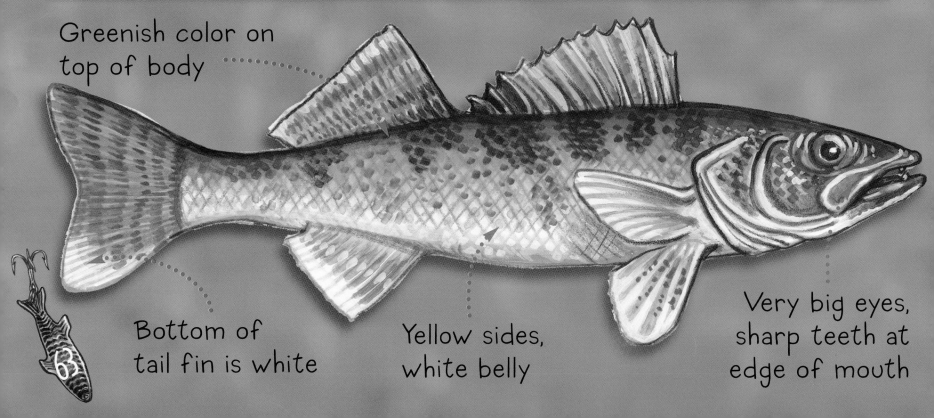

Greenish color on top of body

Bottom of tail fin is white

Yellow sides, white belly

Very big eyes, sharp teeth at edge of mouth

63

YELLOW PERCH

Great taste in a less filling fish.

My Munchies

Minnows

Wigglers

Mousies

My Hangouts

Weedy Beds

Drop-offs

Sticky Piles

The Biggest Ever

4 POUNDS

1/3 POUND

Average Size

How to Catch Me!

Fishermen use spreader rigs with minnows or wigglers. Drop the spreader rig to the bottom and reel in the line so the bait is just off the bottom. Hold the rod still and wait for the perch to take the bait. In water less than fifteen feet deep, beaded jigs are my favorite.

Six or more wide dark stripes running from top to bottom

Short narrow body

Greenish body

Yellow belly, orange fins

LAKE TROUT

My name tells where I live.

My Munchies

Large Minnows

Smelt

Shiners

My Hangouts

Deep Water Lakes

Drop-offs

The Biggest Ever

61 POUNDS

7 POUNDS ← Average Size

How to Catch Me!

A long narrow spoon like a Swedish Pimple baited with a large minnow or smelt jigged right off the bottom in very deep water is a proven method for winter lakers. Bang the jig right on the bottom to get their attention. A live smelt or large minnow fished on a tip-up but also at the bottom of very deep water is also effective.

Greyish to brown body with white spots that extend onto fins

White leading edge on each bottom fin

Large head that is proportionate to body

65

WHITEFISH

My name may not be my color.

My Munchies

Wigglers

Worms

Waxworms

My Hangouts

Deep Water Lakes

Deep Water Holes

The Biggest Ever

14 POUNDS

2.5 POUNDS

Average Size

How to Catch Me!

A plain hook with a waxworm fished on the bottom with very little movement works best. A small chunk of fish spawn (i.e., salmon spawn) on a plain hook fished at the bottom is also very effective. Whitefish have a very soft set of lips and must be pulled in very gingerly to avoid having the hook tear away from their lips.

Top jaw/nose sticks out past bottom jaw

Dark green to deep blue topside

Very small head

Sharply forked tail

66

My Ice Fishing Journal

Date ....

I was at ....

I was with ....

I caught ....

....

I used ....

Date ....

I was at ....

I was with ....

I caught ....

....

I used ....

Date ....

I was at ....

I was with ....

I caught ....

....

I used ....

Date ....

I was at ....

I was with ....

I caught ....

....

I used ....

Date ....

I was at ....

I was with ....

I caught ....

....

I used ....

Date ....

I was at ....

I was with ....

I caught ....

....

I used ....

Date ....

I was at ....

I was with ....

I caught ....

....

I used ....

Date ....

I was at ....

I was with ....

I caught ....

....

I used ....

Date ....

I was at ....

I was with ....

I caught ....
....

I used ....

Date ....

I was at ....

I was with ....

I caught ....
....

I used ....

Date ....

I was at ....

I was with ....

I caught ....
....

I used ....

Date ....

I was at ....

I was with ....

I caught ....
....

I used ....

Date ....

I was at ....

I was with ....

I caught ....
....

I used ....

Date ....

I was at ....

I was with ....

I caught ....
....

I used ....

Date ....

I was at ....

I was with ....

I caught ....
....

I used ....

Date ....

I was at ....

I was with ....

I caught ....
....

I used ....

About the Author

Michael DiLorenzo is passionate about the outdoors and the tremendously valuable experiences and lessons that can be shared by a family on their outdoor treks together. Most of his greatest life experiences have been encountered while outdoors or through the bonds created with friends and family accompanying him on his travels. A married father of three, Michael cherishes his time spent roaming his home state of Michigan, fishing its waters, and hunting its lands on both peninsulas. Bringing others into the outdoors is quickly becoming his favorite pastime.

About Running Moose Publications

Running Moose Publications, the producer of the Adventures with Jonny series, has released this sequel to the original book, *Adventures with Jonny, Let's Go Fishing!* While the first book was based on warm-weather fishing, this second book takes Jonny and friends on a winter fishing trek because fishing is too great an experience to miss out on for six months each year awaiting spring's arrival. The Adventures with Jonny series will continue to expand into other family outdoor activities beyond fishing.

In the next book, slated for release in spring, 2008, Jonny puts his fishing rod aside, grabs the rest of the family, and heads out for an expedition in *Adventures with Jonny, Road Trip to a National Park!* The series is gaining the momentum of a running moose, and how do you stop a running moose…?

About the Illustrator, a Fishy Tale…

As principal artist of Jnnffr Productions (www.jnnffr.com), Jenniffer Julich's passion is visual storytelling and client collaboration. This is the second in the series of Adventures with Jonny books that Jenniffer has designed and illustrated for Mike DiLorenzo. The collaboration and chemistry between writer and illustrator on *Let's Go Fishing!* was so creative that they started the second book in the series while the first book was being printed!

Mike and Jenniffer's rapport brought out humor as well. It's uncommon to get an "art blooper," but one occurred when Jenniffer illustrated the bait "Mousies" as dead baby mice instead of the tailed insects used for bait. The author responded to the artist, "Just to be clear…baits called 'daredevils' have no satanic themes, you cannot actually eat with 'spoons,' 'plugs' cannot stop leaks, and in the future 'Salt Water' edition…a 'hammerhead' is not a tool." The artist replied, "It was the day before April Fool's. If I'd waited to email it only one day later, this could have been magnificently respun."